The Beauty of Golf
in New York State

*C*rag *Burn Golf Club*

Elma
Designers: Robert Trent Jones
            Rees Jones

The Beauty of Golf
in New York State

by John Francis McCarthy

Summerfield House, Ltd. Auburn, New York

Summerfield House, Ltd., Auburn, New York 13021

©1989 by Summerfield House, Ltd.
All rights reserved. Published 1989
Printed in Hong Kong
93 92 91 90 89   5 4 3 2 1

ISBN 0-9623716-0-2

Except as noted in the Contributing Photographers listing on page 98,
all photographs are those of John Francis McCarthy.

Cover design by Chase Design
Book layout and design by Chase Design

*M*onroe Golf Club

Pittsford
Designer: Donald Ross

A long, pleasant journey down the fairways of New York State began for me as a caddie on the slopes of Bellevue Country Club in Syracuse. For teenagers who lived on nearby Tipperary Hill, this was one of our first jobs. My memories of it remain vivid to this day.

Those summer mornings began with the caddie master's call and often ended around the basketball hoop or a card game on slow or rainy days. Words like singles, doubles, tippers, tightwads, woods, irons, birdies, bogies, eagles, aces and par were added to my vocabulary. It was a time when survival in the hot sun often depended on one's ability to gauge and avoid the heaviest leather bags.

I remember the dew sparkling on the greens and the smell of freshly cut grass; blue skies with billowing clouds and Bellevue's panoramic view of the city of Syracuse. Most of all, I remember the camaraderie, the laughter, and the endless anecdotes and stories.

This book was inspired by those memories, to share the aesthetics of a game that words alone cannot describe. For the past three years, I have walked the links of New York and photographed their beauty. From those images, and others I have gathered from fellow photographers, I offer this tribute to the beauty of golf in New York State.

John Francis McCarthy

Auburn, New York 1989

*W*ayne Hills Country Club

Lyons
Designers: Edward L. Packard
          Brent Wadsworth

*I*ntroduction

On the sixth of October, 1656, the Dutch Council of New Netherland issued an ordinance prohibiting the playing of "kolf" in village streets. Kolf, played with a club and a ball and henceforth relegated to the pastures and fields of the Dutch settlement, may well have been the forerunner in New York State of the game we now know as golf.

Others claim that the "greatest game," as Bobby Jones called it, was introduced in New York State in 1887, the result of a gift of golf equipment from Scottish immigrant Robert Lockhart to his friend and fellow Scot, John Reid.

What is known for sure is that in 1888, John Reid founded the first permanent golf club in the United States, St. Andrews in Yonkers, and that Robert Lockhart was its first member.

Within six years, the United States Golf Association was formed. By the turn of the century, golf had captured the imagination of America.

Course designers and golf professionals were rapidly imported from Scotland to plan new courses and instruct novice American golfers. Men like Willie Dunn, Willie Park, Jr., Alister Mackensie, Donald Ross and Charles Blair Macdonald inspired others, including A.W. Tillinghast, William Flynn and Robert Trent Jones, to shape the United States game with a distinctively American design style.

The geography of New York State supplied these imaginative architects with infinite opportunity. Consider the sleepy hollows of the Catskills, the blue distances of the Adirondacks, the sparkle of the Champlain Valley and the long, steep basins of the Finger Lakes. There were, too, the valleys carved by the Mohawk, Allegheny, Susquehanna, Delaware, Hudson and St. Lawrence rivers, and the links-land of the Long Island shore.

The names of New York's courses read like poetry and evoke the history and literature of the region in Dutch, English and the languages of the Iroquois nations. A feeling of tradition is palpable here. One need only examine New York's contribution to the vast collection of golf history and memorabilia on display at Golf House, the Museum and Library of the United States Golf Association in Far Hills, New Jersey, to appreciate the depth of that tradition.

I am grateful to the curator of that collection for the vintage tales with which I've sketched in a bit of the history surrounding many of the courses in this book. For vignettes under which a "USGA Collection" citation appears, I was assisted by Janet Scagle, Librarian and Curator of Golf House. Others who have my special thanks are Norm Boughton of Rochester for a great idea, Richard Donovan, a historian who lives in Endicott, New York, the Metropolitan Golf Association and the New York State Golf Association.

In the parlance of the game, the goal of this book was to walk the courses of New York State in search of photographic aces. So the odyssey proceeded. At many stops along the way, a club pro or enthusiastic player would help by revealing a magical spot as the climax of a scenic ride over acres of perfectly groomed fairways.

The first photographs were taken in Rochester, host city of the 1989 U.S. Open Championship at Oak Hill and site of the International Musem of Photography — an auspicious start.

At Oak Hill, the consensus favored the East course's elevated 13th tee and fairway, sloping gently upward 596 yards to the club's memorable Hill of Fame; at Sleepy Hollow, a little par three overlooking the Catskills and the Hudson at sunset; at Garden City Golf, the "Travis Bunker;" at Albany Country Club, the distant view of the state capital; at Top of the World, the panorama of Lake George, and so on across the state.

The quality and diversity of New York's courses have helped to establish some of the most prestigious golf events in the U.S., including the Metropolitan Open, the Anderson Memorial at Winged Foot, the Travis Memorial at Garden City Golf, and the Porter Cup at Niagara Falls. The state also hosts a number of PGA and LPGA events annually.

Intercity competition, initiated in 1894 by the Tuxedo Club, fostered many regional alliances. One of the oldest of these, the League of the Iroquois (including Wanakah, Oak Hill, Bellevue and Yahnundasis), was established in 1909. The League's invocation reflects the essence of the game:

> Bless thy warriors as the sun shines bright
> On fairway and green with fond recollections
> Of friendships and joyous times past
> And with a continuous spirit
> Of wholesome competition and grand
> companionship.

The same spirit imbues the Empire State's hundred-year heritage of golf. The hope of this book is that, on a rainy or snowy day — or perhaps during a late evening by the fireside — an armchair tour of these beautiful courses will convey some hint of the pleasure, excitement and challenge enjoyed by golfers in the state of New York.

Shinnecock Hills

(right)
Southampton
Designers: Willie Davis
          Willie Dunn, Jr.   Howard Toomey
          William S. Flynn   William F. Mitchell

Shinnecock Hills was the first incorporated golf club in the country and the first 18-hole course. It is named for the Shinnecocks, an Algonquin tribe that once hunted and fished from Shinnecock Bay to Montauk along the southern shore of Long Island. Shinnecock Indians, supervised by the designer, helped construct the course on their ancestral territory.

The question of who designed the original Shinnecock Hills course is the subject of a lively detective story by Robert Sommers, editor of the United States Golf Association's *Golf Journal*. In that publication's March/April 1987 issue, Sommers asks, "Which Willie Done It?" — Willie Dunn, Jr., the famous architect credited by many with the job, or Willie Davis, Dunn's contemporary and rival? Illustrating the article is a photo of the pair sitting side by side after a tournament which Davis had won at the Lennox Golf Club in Massachusetts.

Willie Dunn took credit for the Shinnecock Hills course in an interview published in *Golf Illustrated* in 1934. However, in a letter written 40 years earlier to a British golf magazine, the Scotsman indicated that his first visit to the U.S. wasn't until 1893 — two years after the course was designed — and the letter did not mention Shinnecock Hills in a list of his courses.

According to the club's history, Shinnecock Hills was designed in 1891 by a gentleman on leave from the Royal Montreal Golf Club. Sommers cites a request in the minutes of the Montreal club, located by the curator of the Royal Canadian Golf Association Museum, from several Long Islanders "for the loan of their professional, Willie Davis, in order to design a course and instruct them in how to play the game."

Which Willie, indeed?

Photo: ©Jules Alexander

Oswego Country Club

Oswego
Designer: A.W. Tillinghast

*B*riarwood Country Club

Hamburg

*T*he Nevele Hotel

Ellenville
Designers: Alfred H. Tull
George Fazio
Tom Fazio

In the late 1800's, the story goes, eleven local school teachers went on a picnic in the woods. They came upon a waterfall so perfect that they decided to name it after their own group, by spelling the word "eleven" backwards. The Nevele Hotel was later founded on that very waterfall site. On the edge of the course stands a refurbished red and white schoolhouse once attended by the resort's founder.

*B*urnet Park

Syracuse
Designer: Larry Murphy

*O*wasco Country Club

Auburn

St. Andrews Golf Club

Hastings-on-Hudson
Designers: William Tucker, Sr.   Jack Nicklaus
             James Braid   Bob Cupp

St. Andrews is America's oldest golf club in continuous operation. The wanderings of its founders, known as the "Old Apple Tree Gang," traced a continual improvement in sites on which to enjoy golf.

They first played on three improvised holes in a Yonkers cow pasture. Shortly thereafter, they moved to a 30-acre, six-hole course preempted from the local butcher, then to an apple orchard from which the "Gang" got its name, and later to Grey Oaks in the Sawmill River valley before finally settling in Mt. Hope.

In the apple orchard, one tree which stood near the first

tee and the home green became an integral part of the club itself, serving all the purposes of a 19th hole. On its limbs the players hung their coats, an ample lunch basket, and an old wicker demijohn which provided Scotland's favorite thirst quencher. Thus provisioned, the Gang would happily pass an entire day, from morning until nightfall, at their beloved game.

From *St. Andrews Golf Club 1888-1938* by H.B. Martin and A.B. Halliday (USGA Collection)

Piping Rock Club

Locust Valley
Designers: C.B. Macdonald
             Seth Raynor

*S*hadow Lake

Penfield
Designer: Gordon Odenbach

6

*S*hadow Pines Golf Club

Penfield
Designer: Gordon Odenbach

Rip Van Winkle Golf & Country Club

(left)
Palenville
Designer: Donald Ross

Located in a small village in the foothills of the Catskill Mountains, this course nestles in the area where the character Rip Van Winkle slept for 20 years in Washington Irving's famous nineteenth-century tale.

During the Roaring Twenties, one of the club's most colorful characters was Marty Casey, a flamboyant accountant who drove a Packard convertible, owned countless pairs of expensive shoes, and had a fondness for strong liquor.

But style was no match for skill. On the course, Casey was easily bested by "the Judge," as fellow member and Ulster County Surrogate George Kaufman was known. Kaufman, a self-taught golfer who practiced relentlessly to hone his accuracy, would spend entire afternoons hitting bag after bag of balls — dropping every one within just a step or two of the caddie he posted on the fairway to retrieve them.

From *The Rip Van Winkle Golf & Country Club: A Historical Recollection* by Albert G. Naudain, 1979

Green Lakes State Park Golf Course

Fayetteville
Designers: Robert Trent Jones
William F. Mitchell

*W*akely Lodge Golf Club

Indian Lake

*C*lifton Springs Country Club

Clifton Springs
Designer: Pete Craig

Alone on the course, this golfer was gracious enough
to move his ball to the difficult lie in which I asked to
photograph him. He even volunteered to attempt a
shot. When I replied that that wouldn't be necessary,
he assured me, "No, really, I'm used to these kinds of
shots!"

*I*BM Country Club

Poughkeepsie
Designer: Robert Trent Jones

The shot hit the pin!

*A*ttica Golf Club

Attica

S *iwanoy Country Club*

Bronxville
Designers: Donald Ross
           Tom Winton   William G. Robinson
           Geoffrey S. Cornish   Robert Trent Jones

The first PGA Championship was held at Siwanoy in 1916. It was won by Jim Barnes, who sank a four-foot putt to win $500 in cash, a diamond-studded gold medal, custody of the huge silver Wanamaker Trophy, the professional championship title and the status of leading professional of the season.

Almost as noteworthy, though, are the famous "Snobirds of Siwanoy." According to Snobird president Joel Parker, the object of the organization, founded in 1908, is to promote wintertime golf. The regular course is played when the weather is fair and the chairman of the Green Committee approves. However, a special nine-hole Snobird course is always ready in case snow, ice or sleet puts the regular course off limits. Here, the greens are of sand, the flags are brooms for sweeping them, and special rules govern play from traps and rough. Retired "Rocking Chair Snobirds" watch the competition from the warm and cheery confines of the Grill, as they swap tales of memorable Snobird tournaments in years gone by.

From *The Seventy-Fifth Anniversary: Siwanoy Country Club 1901-1976* (USGA Collection)

Woodcliff Golf Course

Fairport
Designer: Gordon Odenbach

Normanside Country Club

(right)
Delmar
Designer: William Harries

The Normanside Country Club is located beside the
Normanskill, or valley of Tawasentha, a place made
famous by Henry Wadsworth Longfellow in the verse
introduction to his poem, "The Song of Hiawatha" —
    In the vale of Tawasentha
    In the green and silent valley,
    By the pleasant water-courses,
    Dwelt the singer Nawadaha.

    Round about the Indian village
    Spread the meadows and the cornfields,
    And beyond them stood the forest,
    Stood the groves of singing pine trees,
    Green in summer, white in winter,
    Ever sighing, ever singing.

*I*rondequoit Country Club

Rochester
Designer: J.B. McGovern

*O*ld Oaks Country Club

Purchase
Designers: Charles Hugh Alison   Frank Duane
            H.S. Colt   William Newcomb
            William F. Mitchell   Stephen Kay

*M*assena Country Club

(left)
Massena
Designer: Albert H. Murray

*S*tonehedge Golf Course

Groton

In a cemetery plot east of Stonehedge's sixth green,
Abijah Virgil, a Revolutionary War veteran, is buried.
Private Virgil, who was captured and held for a year
in a British prison in Canada, served in the Battle of
Princeton, the Battle of Saratoga and the taking of
British General Burgoyne. His tombstone reads:
>   In early life my country call'd
>   And I its voice obeyed
>   By foes my body was enthrall'd
>   And now in earth is laid.

Contributed by American Legion Carrington-Fuller
Post 800, Groton

*M*ark Twain Golf Course

Elmira
Designer: Donald Ross

Mark Twain is said to have attempted to visit an old friend who was a U.S. Senator, while the senator was playing golf. Twain walked the course, searching for him, until he heard shocking language wafted by the breeze from beyond a hillock. Clambering up, Twain watched his friend trying in vain to whack his ball out of a frightfully deep pit. After a while the senator saw him. "Hello, Sam!" said the senator.

Gazing down into the hellish place where his friend seemed destined to spend eternity, Twain replied, "Hello, Dante!"

From "The Humor of the Game" by A.W. Tillinghast, *Golf Illustrated*, March 1915

*H*oliday Valley

Ellicottville

*I*nlet Golf Course

Inlet

According to Roland Christy, course professional and manager, deer are plentiful at this Adirondack site, and even bear are occasionally seen on the links. Christy, in fact, once had to order additional flag sticks after a bear broke several during an evening tour of the greens.

From *Adirondack Golf Courses...Past and Present* by J. Peter Martin, Lake Placid, 1987

*W*anakah Country Club

Buffalo
Designers: Bob Cupp
          Jay Morrish

_M_alone Golf Club

Malone
Designers: Willard Wilkinson
           Albert Murray

During the fall of 1903, the golf pioneers of Malone improvised a course at the local fairground race track with greens on the infield and outfield, and the turf and fences as hazards. A few months later, a true par 38, 2430-yard, nine-hole course was laid out. The annual fee for limited membership was five dollars.

In 1935, the Town of Malone agreed to apply for a federal WPA grant to help finance new plans for a nine-hole course and clubhouse. When the new course opened, baseball great Babe Ruth was a member of the first foursome. Historian Mabel Hawley wrote: "The course was formally opened by Babe Ruth on

July 1, 1939. It was a rainy day, but...a gallery of 200 followed. Ruth tied for honors in the match with a 37 score. The greens were not too smooth and the Babe remarked he needed a niblick to play them. It was then decided to play onto the green and count two strokes for sinking putts. Number five was a short par 3 hole, but the green was very large. When Babe was told his drive was on the green, he asked his caddie for his brassie because the ball was so far from the cup and he wanted a birdie to break the tie."

From _A History of The Malone Golf Course_ by Ray Russell and Helen Russell, 1987

20

Garden City Golf Club

(left)
Garden City
Designers: Devereux Emmet   Robert Trent Jones
           Walter J. Travis   Frank Duane

The Garden City links impressed the USGA so favorably that the 1900 Amateur Championship was held there. It was won by Walter Travis, a 39-year-old Garden City member, who had played the game for a mere four seasons.

For the next three years, Travis was unquestionably the country's leading amateur golfer. He captured the Amateur Championship again in 1901 and 1903. In 1904, he entered the British Amateur Championship at the Royal St. George in Sandwich. This tournament, the blue-ribbon event of the amateur golf world, had never been won by a foreigner.

In practice rounds over a number of links, Travis shot poorly and made few friends among the British golfers. By the time the match was to be played, however, he was beginning to emerge from his slump, except for the putting on which he relied heavily.

An American friend urged Travis to try a new type of putter called the "Schenectady," recently designed by Arthur T. Knight of the General Electric Company. The club had a mallet-shaped head made of aluminum with the shaft placed in the center. The new putter restored Travis's confidence.

With icy resentment, the British galleries watched the drama unfold. Reluctantly, they conceded Travis's genius, as he became the first American to win a major British title. The official reaction of the Royal and Ancient, however, was to outlaw center-shaft putters for many years to come.

After retiring from tournament competition, Travis established himself as an expert in course architecture. This photograph captures Garden City pro Gil McNally in the infamous Travis-style bunker. When Travis added the original six-foot deep bunker, there was considerable opposition from the members, but the "Old Man" stubbornly defended it.

From *The Garden City Golf Club 1899-1974* by
Neal Fulkerson and John Thacher (USGA Collection)

Blue Heron Hills Country Club

Macedon

The Tuxedo Club

(right)
Tuxedo Park
Designers: Robert Trent Jones
            Frank Duane

Long ago, Tuxedo Park was an uninhabited wilderness between great Indian nations, the Algonquins to the east and south, and the Six Nations of the Iroquois to the north and east.

Today, the only traces of these hunting tribes are the smoke stains left on the rocks by their fires and the name they gave to the lake, Ptucksepo. The first white settlers attempted to convert this into such Anglicisms as "Duck Sider" or "Duck Cedar," but eventually the Indian name "Tuxedo" won out.

The Tuxedo Club was the first to suggest an intercity team match. Late in the summer of 1894, just after St. Andrews had announced its intention to hold an amateur championship, Tuxedo sent out invitations to St. Andrews, Shinnecock Hills, and Brookline to determine which club had the best players.

The best golfers in the country gathered for the match play. In a memorable match at St. Andrews, all but L.B. Stoddard of the host club and the renowned Charles B. Macdonald of Chicago were eliminated. Macdonald lost the match after hitting into a plowed rough. Had there been an out-of-bounds rule like today's, he would have lost only one stroke and the results might have been different.

Stoddard was hailed as the Champion of the United States, but Macdonald protested against an "official" title with no sanctioning organization behind it. Although the Easterners sniffed that Macdonald should have objected before the championship was played, his complaint may well have hastened the formation of the United States Golf Association.

From *The Tuxedo Club 1886-1986* and *St. Andrews Golf Club 1888-1938* by H.B. Martin and A.B. Halliday (USGA Collection)

Brae Burn Golf Course

Dansville

Garrison Golf Club

(left)
Garrison-on-Hudson
Designer: Dick Wilson

On a crisp autumn day, the sounds of drumming, rifle practice and a ceremonial cannon echo from West Point across the Hudson Valley to the fairways of Garrison Golf Club, which stretch along the crest of Fort Hill and curve down into hardwood-covered valleys.

Originally named North Redoubt Country Club, the property was first used as a center for rehabilitating wealthy people with alcohol dependencies. The name North Redoubt came from the Revolutionary War, when pickets were posted above the fort at West Point to spot British ships sneaking up the Hudson for surprise attacks.

Nowadays, the only attack might be the putting yips. Garrison's greens are fast and slippery. But even though golfers may not always shoot to their handicaps, the views and challenge make a round memorable and worthwhile. William Davis' book, *100 Greatest Courses And Then Some* lists Garrison as an undiscovered gem. A gem, indeed, it is.

David Earl, Managing Editor, *Golf Illustrated*, 1989

Whiteface Resort and Country Club

Lake Placid
Designer: John Van Kleek

The first photograph ever to appear on the front page of the New York Times was of Rosa Ponselle, a former Metropolitan Opera star who was hit by a golf ball while playing at Whiteface. This story and many others about the golf courses of the Adirondacks can be found in a book by Whiteface golf professional J. Peter Martin, titled *Adirondack Golf Courses...Past and Present*.

For years, Martin jotted down the tales of oldtimers in the Lake Placid area; some recalled games on courses that had been closed or deserted for over 80 years. In time, the collection grew to encompass the entire Adirondack Park region. These stories trace the development of golf in a part of the state where such renowned architects as Donald Ross, Seymour Dunn, Willie Dunn and Alex Findlay laid memorable foundations for the game.

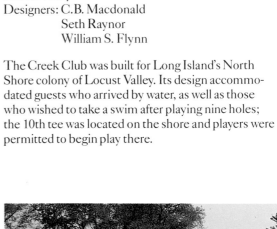

*C*reek Club

Locust Valley
Designers: C.B. Macdonald
           Seth Raynor
           William S. Flynn

The Creek Club was built for Long Island's North Shore colony of Locust Valley. Its design accommodated guests who arrived by water, as well as those who wished to take a swim after playing nine holes; the 10th tee was located on the shore and players were permitted to begin play there.

*C*arlowden

Denmark

*W*indham Country Club

Windham
Designer: Hal Purdy

*T*hendara Golf Club

Old Forge
Designer: Donald Ross

*W*inged Foot Golf Course

Mamaroneck
Designers: A.W. Tillinghast
           Robert Trent Jones   George Fazio
           Dick Wilson   Tom Fazio

The idea for Winged Foot was proposed in 1920 by a small group of members of the New York Athletic Club in Manhattan's Central Park South. They felt that another golf course was needed in the metropolitan area. The name of the club is derived from the sculpture of Mercury, the fleet-footed Roman deity represented as a young man with winged sandals in a statue in the NYAC lobby.

In the 1929 U.S. Open at Winged Foot, Bobby Jones dropped six strokes in five holes, then sank a 12-foot putt over curving terrain to force a playoff with Al Espinosa. The next day, Jones won the playoff. A year later, he won the Grand Slam of golf: the British Open, the British Amateur, the U.S. Amateur and the U.S. Open. It was the first time anyone captured all four titles in a single year.

From *Winged Foot Story: The Golf, The People, The Friendly Trees* by Douglas LaRue Smith, 1984

*B*inghamton Country Club

Binghamton
Designers: A.W. Tillinghast
           William Gordon
           David Gordon

27

*L*ocust Hill Country Club

Rochester
Designers: Seymour Dunn
            Robert Trent Jones

*E*ast Aurora Country Club

East Aurora
Designers: William Harries
        A. Russell Tryon

Craig Wood Golf Club

(right)
Lake Placid
Designer: Seymour Dunn

Once known as the Lake Placid Country Club, this golf course was renamed in the early 1950's to honor a native son. Craig R. Wood, considered one of the longest hitters ever to play the game, won both the U.S. Open and the Masters in 1941.

From *Adirondack Golf Courses...Past and Present* by J. Peter Martin, Lake Placid, 1987

Inwood Country Club

Inwood
Designers: Dr. William Exton
        Arthur Thatcher   Hal Purdy
        Herbert Strong   Frank Duane

In the year 1900, a prominent tobacco merchant named Jacob Wertheim was engaged to a woman who liked golf but had no place to play. Wertheim decided that he would build his ladylove a golf course.

Forthwith, he and two associates rented a potato farm at Inwood, Long Island, where they converted an old farm building into a club house and called it Inwood Country Club.

In 1901, William Martin, the club pro, received an annual fee of two hundred dollars for his services. In 1902, Martin took a job driving a cab.

Two decades later, the esteemed Inwood Country Club hosted the 1923 U.S. Golf Open Championship, where Bobby Jones unleashed what was called "the shot of the century." It was the playoff round, and Jones and Bobby Cruickshank had reached the final hole with identical medal scores.

Cruickshank hit first, hooking his drive into the rough on the right side of the fairway. He had to play his second shot short of the water. Jones, too, pushed his tee shot into the rough on the right side of the fairway. His ball had a depressed lie; the shot would be a difficult one. Jones had a choice to make. If he played short of the water he and Cruickshank would have an equal chance to chip up for a possible par four. If he elected to go for the green and the ball hit the water, he would certainly lose.

Jones selected a two iron, addressed the ball and swung. The ball landed within six feet of the cup, and with his third and final stroke, the 21-year-old won the first of his many national championships.

From *Seventy-Fifth Anniversary: Inwood Country Club 1901-1976* (USGA Collection)

The Country Club of Rochester

(left)
Rochester
Designers: Donald Ross   Arthur Hills
           Robert Trent Jones   Steve Forrest

It was 1913, the year Donald Ross's plans for a new 18-hole course design were approved by the Country Club of Rochester. The club's youthful professional, who had spent his boyhood caddying and making clubs in the pro shop, approached the Green Committee with a request for some time off. He wanted to go to Brookline, Massachusetts, for four or five days to compete in the U.S. Open Golf Championship. The committee, who expected professionals — especially young, unknown ones — to stay on the job, did not heartily endorse the idea.

But Walter Hagen's request was granted and he went to Brookline. After 72 holes, Ted Ray and Harry Varden, the crack British golfers, were tied with a young New Englander named Francis Quimet, who was the sensation of the tournament. Quimet finally won the three-way playoff and the nation's accolades. Except for the ecstatic club members to whom he returned, no one paid much attention to the newcomer from Rochester who had finished fourth in his first tournament, posting the second lowest score at the end of regulation play.

But Hagen resolved to teach the other professionals a lesson, having been, he felt, badly treated by the celebrities who had never heard of him. "They pushed me off the tee and told me I could practice when they got through," he said. "I'm going back next year and win that tournament."

The following year, Walter Hagen indeed entered and won the National Open in Chicago. For the young Rochester native, it was the beginning of a virtually undisputed 20-year reign over professional golf in the U.S. and abroad.

From *The Country Club of Rochester Through Half a Century,* 1945 (USGA Collection)

©MGA Collection

Old Westbury Golf & Country Club

Old Westbury
Designers: William F. Mitchell
            Joseph S. Finger

*A*pawamis Club

Rye
Designers: Willie Davis
Willie Dunn, Jr.   Tom Bendelow
Maturin Ballou   Alfred H. Tull
Tom Winton   George Fazio
Peter W. Lees   Tom Fazio

Among the oldest incorporated clubs in the country, Apawamis was the scene of the 1911 National Amateur Championship won by Harold Hilton over Fred Herreshoff on the 37th hole. Hilton won the day when his poorly-played second shot hit a large protruding rock (now known as Hilton's Rock) in the woods and bounded within 18 inches of the cup.

From *Golf Illustrated*, December 1933 (USGA Collection)

*L*ake Placid Club

Lake Placid
Designers: Seymour Dunn
 Alexander H. Findlay
 Alister Mackensie

*S*tamford Golf Club

Stamford

*C*atatonk Golf Club

Candor
Designer: Hal Purdy

*F*illmore Golf Club

Moravia

36

Westchester Country Club

(left)
Rye
Designer: Walter J. Travis

John McEntee Bowman, founder and builder of the Westchester-Biltmore, later to become the Westchester Country Club, emigrated from Toronto to New York City with nothing to his name but carfare. Twenty years later, he was president of the Bowman-Biltmore Hotels, one of the world's largest chains.

At Westchester, Bowman gave shape to his vision of an ideal community for millionaire sportsmen and an outstanding year-round resort for wealthy travelers.

The design of the club's championship West Course, as a result, had a unique feature: it was reversible. During the winter, to preserve the greens while enjoying off-season golf whenever the weather permitted, players were allowed to use the broad tees as greens and play the course backwards!

Members in those days were advised that "golf is now as necessary an accomplishment as the piano. Start your kids with your golf teachers and get them going right so that in the future they may be in the 70 class."

But if the youngsters were looking to their elders for an example, they witnessed some strange sights. For instance, there was the player whose Herculean efforts to blast his ball from a sand trap lost him his set of teeth.

And there was George McCarthy, a golfer with a wicked hook. One day he set his ball on the first tee of the South Course, swung, and off it went flying through a window into the main dining room, narrowly missing a bowl of soup and a glass of iced coffee on a table where two other members were sitting.

Undaunted, McCarthy calmly opened the doors of the dining room, cleared the way and made a chip shot from the carpet. He got the ball out of the dining room, all right, but it hit a tree and rebounded onto the terrace. Whereupon McCarthy, with his trusty brassie, made a beautiful shot to the fairway and on to the first green.

From *Defending the Dream: A Fifty-Year History of the Triumphs and Vicissitudes of the Westchester Country Club — John Bowman's Unique Creation* by Dorothy Fine, Irwin Fredman and Fred Jarvis, 1979

Ausable Club Golf Course

St. Huberts
Designer: Seymour Dunn

The Ausable Club, known at one time as the Adirondack Mountain Reserve, was formed in 1887 to offer golf in a unique setting that closely harmonized with the "forever wild" character of the neighboring forest land.

*S*aratoga Spa Championship Golf Course

Saratoga Springs
Designer: William F. Mitchell

*S*pook Rock Golf Course

Ramapo
Designer: Frank Duane

40

*T*eugega Country Club

(left)
Rome
Designers: Donald Ross
William F. Mitchell

"Teugega" is the name the Iroquois gave to the Mohawk River. The original Teugega golf course was situated on the banks of the Mohawk until shortly after World War I.

Apparently the name of the club was a controversial subject from the beginning. In 1921, while the new course was being built on Lake Delta, "the name 'Teugega' had a fight for its life but was retained", recalls a club chronicle.

When the first course was built on the river's edge, "the question came up as to what to call this club. Here is where Eugene Rowland came in. He was easily the most literary member of this intrepid band and he had somewhere discovered in his Indian legends this name of 'Teugega' which none of us could pronounce and cannot even to this day. Eugene said it meant something impressive...I've forgotten what it was. It might have been 'parting of the waters' because the waters flow two ways from [Rome] into the gulf of the St. Lawrence to the west and the Hudson River to the east."

From *Fifty Years at Teugega Country Club*

*B*rae Burne Country Club

Purchase
Designer: Frank Duane

Cornell University Golf Club

Ithaca
Designer: Robert Trent Jones

When Robert Trent Jones attended Cornell University from 1928 to 1930 as a special student in the School of Agriculture, no specific curriculum in golf course architecture was offered, so Jones was allowed to plan his own studies. He took classes in surveying, hydraulics, landscape architecture, horticulture, and agronomy. He also studied journalism, public speaking and art, with an emphasis on sketching that proved invaluable in his design work.

Jones returned to Cornell in 1954 to add a second nine holes to the course which he had designed in 1941. In 1983, he was inducted into the university's Athletic Hall of Fame.

From the Cornell University Sports Information Office

Fallsview Hotel Golf Course

Ellenville
Designer: Robert Trent Jones

Loon Lake Golf Course

Loon Lake

Chili Country Club

Scottsville

Bethpage State Park Golf Course

Farmingdale
Designers: A.W. Tillinghast
         Frank Duane
         Alfred H. Tull

In the Bible, Bethphage or "House of Figs" is located between Jericho and Jerusalem. The Long Island community with a modern spelling of that name was acquired from the Indians by Thomas Powell, the area's first white settler. According to Harrison Hunt, Curator of American History for Nassau County's Museum Division, the villages established after Powell's deal with the Indians included Farmingdale, Central Park (plans for a Central Park in Manhattan were also underway), and the hamlet of Bethpage. When the state acquired the land in the early 1930's and built Bethpage State Park, the two villages that by then had a railroad station and post office, Farmingdale and Central Park, competed to be renamed Bethpage. Central Park won, ceding its original name to the Manhattan greensward for good. The hamlet of Bethpage, in turn, became Old Bethpage.

Today, the state park's back course is considered one of the finest public golf courses in America.

Ardsley Country Club

(right)
Ardsley-on-Hudson
Designers: Willie Dunn, Jr.   William H. Tucker
          Alister Mackensie   Stephen Kay

Located above the Hudson River on estates once owned by John Jacob Astor and Cyrus W. Field, Ardsley is the third oldest country club in the United States. It was the site of the first USGA women's tournament, played in 1898; Miss Beatrix Hoyt defeated Miss Maude Wetmore, 5 and 3.

Originally called the Ardsley Casino on the "American Rhine," the club was built by prominent New Yorkers including William Rockefeller, Edwin Gould, Alfred Vanderbilt and J.P. Morgan "for the development and improvement of literary and social intercourse, and for the physical and mental cultivation of its members." Architect Willie Dunn considered his work at Ardsley "a masterpiece of golf construction work."

From *Ardsley Country Club 1885-1955* by Albert E. Koehl (USGA Collection)

McGregor Links Country Club

Saratoga Springs
Designer: Devereux Emmet

McGregor Links owes its existence to a gentleman who never played the game. Edgar T. Brackett, a former New York State Senator, built the 800-acre course to add an extra attraction to the already famous health and recreational facilities of Saratoga Springs.

©Linda Bishop McCarthy

*L*ake Placid Club

Lake Placid
Designers: Seymour Dunn
Alexander H. Findlay
Alister Mackensie

The Lake Placid Club was established in 1895 largely through the efforts of Melvil Dewey, inventor of the Dewey Decimal System. The original membership consisted of 30 people who resided on the five-acre estate, but by the early 1900's it had developed into a full-scale resort of 1200 acres that could easily accommodate 1000 members and guests.

Seymour Dunn, one of golf's best teaching professionals, was director of golf at Lake Placid for 21 years. Dunn was also a club maker, architect and author, as well as Adirondack Open Champion for 12 years in succession.

From *Adirondack Golf Courses...Past and Present* by J. Peter Martin, Lake Placid, 1987

*C*avalry Club

(right)
Manlius
Designers: Dick Wilson
Joe Lee

From the Cavalry Club's terrace overlooking the finishing green and adjacent pond, a different kind of golf game is often played. It goes like this: each spectator bets on which player in the foursome approaching the 18th green will hole out first. The ball must be putted in; "gimmies" are not allowed.

On one particularly hot and humid August day, after four- or five-putting the green and in full view of the terrace, a frustrated player hurled his clubs, bag and all, into the pond. The wager on holing out was forgotten in a frenzy of betting on the time it would take the irate golfer to cool off and retrieve his clubs. All bets were off, however, when after 15 minutes or so, the gentleman returned with shoes and socks in hand to wade out to the bag, retrieve only his car keys, and then toss the bag even farther into the pond.

48

Top of the World

(left)
Lake George
Designer: Charles Tuttle

Top of the World was built on French Mountain, whose name recalls the French soldiers who escaped across it after an unsuccessful attack on Fort Henry during the French and Indian War. From here on a clear day, golfers can see nearly 90 miles to Mount Marcy, New York's highest peak.

From *Adirondack Golf Courses...Past and Present* by J. Peter Martin, Lake Placid, 1987

Corning Country Club

Corning
Designer: Thomas Winton

The Corning Classic is a major benefit event on the annual LPGA tour. Since the inaugural tournament in 1979, hospitals in the southern tier have received over a million dollars in tournament proceeds.

In the photo, club pro Charlie Keating stands beside a sundial donated in his honor by the Houghton family of Corning in 1980, to commemorate his 40 years of service to the club.

*A*lbany Country Club

Guilderland
Designer: Robert Trent Jones

*I*BM Country Club

Johnson City
Designer: Geoffrey S. Cornish

51

Livingston Country Club

Geneseo

Brookfield Country Club

Clarence
Designer: William Harries

Pinehaven Country Club

Guilderland
Designer: Armaund Farina

Pinehaven is located in New York State's protected Pinebush area. It is one of the earliest upstate clubs to open each year and often the last to close, thanks to the speedy drainage provided by the course's sand base.

Lakeside Country Club

Penn Yan

Bluff Point Golf & Country Club

Plattsburgh
Designer: A.W. Tillinghast

When Dorothy Campbell Hurd won the Women's
International Invitation Tournament at Bluff Point in
1934, she remarked that it was her 750th golf prize.
She had won her first at the age of 12, but even then
was already a seasoned competitor, having entered her
first tournament at five years of age. That tournament
"didn't amount to much," she said. "I just played until I
got tired and then I was carried the rest of the way."

From *Golf Illustrated*, October 1934

Maidstone Club

(right)
East Hampton
Designers: William Tucker, Sr.
Perry Maxwell C. Wheaton Vaughan
Willie Park, Jr. Alfred H. Tull

East Hampton's earliest English settlers arrived in 1648 from Maidstone in Kent, and at first, they called their New World settlement Maidstone. Two and a half centuries later, their descendants gave the same name to the course on which they again harked back to British roots — this time by playing the game of golf.

Bellevue Country Club

Syracuse
Designers: Donald Ross
Willard Wilkinson
Frank Duane

Syracuse newspaper columnist Joe Ganley remembers the day in 1927 when U.S. Open Champion Tommy Armour and Walter Hagen arrived at Bellevue to play an exhibition. Ganley, on his way to the kitchen with a dime and his good looks to buy a sandwich, approached Armour and asked if he could give him a hand with his bag. Armour told the hungry kid to get his shoes out of the bag for him, which Ganley rushed to do.

The boy's search, however, proved futile. Armour, muttering something about Ganley's ancestors, magically whisked open a sort of secret compartment and retrieved the shoes himself. Then Walter Hagen, who had observed the exchange from nearby, walked over to Ganley and said, "Here kid, let me show you something. It's a newfangled thing called a zipper."

Skaneateles Country Club

(left)
Skaneateles
Designer: Hal Purdy

On the wall in the grill at this beautiful club overlooking
Skaneateles Lake hangs a copy of a scroll presented to
former club pro John Loss "in recognition of his superb
skill as a golfer as is evidenced by his amazing and
phenomenal score of 26 for nine holes of golf played
at the Skaneateles Country Club on June 10, 1955."

John Loss's score card read:

Hole	1	2	3	4	5	6	7	8	9	Total
Par	3	5	4	3	5	3	5	4	4	36
Loss	1	3	3	3	3	2	4	4	3	26

Niagara Falls Country Club

Niagara Falls
Designers: William Newcomb
        Robert Trent Jones

The Woodmere Club

Great Neck
Designers: Jack Pirie
        Gil Nicholls   Robert Trent Jones

58

*C*ortland Country Club

Cortland
Designer: Willard Wilkinson

*S*odus Bay Heights Golf Club

Sodus Point
Designers: Robert Trent Jones
          Geoffrey S. Cornish
          William G. Robinson

*S*tafford Country Club

Stafford
Designer: Walter J. Travis

*S*aratoga Golf & Polo Club

Saratoga Springs

*M*cConnellsville Golf Club

McConnellsville

*W*omen on a Mission

By 1890, American women had taken up golf; playing a fast game soon became a swank pastime among them. Women's sporting attire began to favor Scottish tweeds, the better to step into the rough. Considerable fanfare attended their first national title play, held in 1895.

As H.L. Fitspatrick reported in *Outing Magazine*, "The first links to be graced by women on such a mission was Meadowbrook on Long Island, where on a misty drizzling morning in the late fall of 1895, a baker's dozen met to compete for the title and a silver cup.

"This course...one of the longest nine-holes in the country...was quite unsuited to test the skill of the competitors, who had learned on much easier links. The winner was Mrs. Charles S. Brown from Shinnecock Hills, while Miss Nina Sargent from Essex Country Club, who had luck on one or two holes, was second. Mrs. Brown...walked into the Meadowbrook clubhouse with a scorecard which totaled 132 for 18 holes of medal play.

"'Don't twit me!' Mrs. Brown cautioned the friend who told her she was the champion. 'I know my limit, but it was fun playing anyway.'"

Although the modest Mrs. Brown at first disclaimed the honor, the engraved silver cup (now a part of the United States Golf Association collection) attests to her win with the inscription: "Ladies Golf Champion, November 9, 1895, Lucy Barnes Brown."

*G*olf Club of Newport

Newport
Designers: Geoffrey S. Cornish
William G. Robinson

Newman Golf Course

(right)
Ithaca

Tupper Lake Golf Club

Tupper Lake
Designer: Donald Ross

Sporting Advice

Some years ago, an upstate sportscaster signed off his broadcasts with the advice: "Remember…whether you win or lose, always be a good sport."

As one story goes, this media star once hit a beautiful drive only to miss a short putt for a birdie, and then without warning proceeded to strike the green with such force that the head of his putter disappeared from sight.

His caddie, showing either the wisdom he'd gained from those broadcasts or the confidence that he could dodge a forcefully wielded putter, soberly admonished the sportscaster to "Remember…"

*E*n-Joie Country Club

Endicott
Designers: Ernest E. Smith   Pete Dye
           William F. Mitchell   David Postlethwaite

En-Joie was built by George F. Johnson, president of the Endicott-Johnson Corporation, for the enjoyment and benefit of his employees. Johnson, a sportsman and philanthropist, took care to assure that this beautiful course would be both accessible and pleasurable to those for whom it was designed.

He fixed a nominal greens fee of 25 cents, a figure within reach of the employees' pocketbooks. He also acquired several thousand golf clubs and golf bags of assorted kinds and sizes, which employees could purchase at a dollar for a club and two dollars and 50 cents for a bag.

And finally, Johnson sent a committee of 12 experts from his factory — the source of a large share of the world's rubber soles and heels — to find out how the finest golf balls were made. When they returned, Johnson diversified into golf ball manufacturing on a major scale.

His philosophy even influenced the original course design. He felt that the simplest course would be challenging enough for a beginner, and that employees had neither the time to spend looking for balls nor the money to squander in losing them. So the builders were advised to include as few traps and as little rough as possible.

Today's more challenging course is the result of remodeling by William F. Mitchell in the late 1930's and by Pete Dye and David Postlethwaite in 1984.

"A love and pursuit of outdoor sports is one of the finest and most important developments of recent times," Johnson declared in the old days, "and I place golf at the top of these. It not only renders real physical benefits, but it yields greater zest for the enjoyment of life, and incidentally for work."

From "Big Business in the Bunkers: George F. Johnson Gets His Boys Out Of The Rough" by Tracy Hammond Lewis, *American Golfer*, July 1929

*O*neonta Country Club

Oneonta
Designer: William E. Harries

James Baird State Park

(right)
Pleasant Valley
Designer: Robert Trent Jones

The Lincoln Memorial and the Folger Shakespeare
Memorial Library in Washington are among the
famous institutions built by the prominent contractor,
James Baird. This golf course was built by the Civilian
Conservation Corps in 1939 on farm land donated by
Baird to the state.

Saranac Lake Golf Club

Raybrook
Designers: Alexander H. Findlay
        Scott North

*T*he Park Club

(right)
Buffalo
Designers: H.S. Colt   Arthur Hills
           C.H. Allison   Steve Forrest

The Park Club, the second oldest organization in the Buffalo district, was incorporated for "lawful exhibitions and contests in driving automobiles and other riding and driving, golfing, tennis, basketball, baseball, skating and all other lawful sports."

The Park Club first convened at the clubhouse and grounds of the former Country Club of Buffalo, which had been vacated to make way for the Pan-American Exposition of 1901. The Exposition's decorative canals were converted to water hazards, and a large mound, built as part of an American Indian exhibit, became a bunker on the first hole.

Milton W. Mugler, president of the club in 1945, was once featured in Ripley's "Believe It or Not" for a hole-in-one that "never touched the green." Even more exciting, though, was the 1934 PGA Championship held at the Park Club, with Paul Runyon of the Metropolis Country Club in White Plains defeating Craig Wood, the longest hitter on the tour, in a sudden-death playoff.

From *The Park Club of Buffalo 1903-1978* by Edward T. Dunn, S.J., 1978 (USGA Collection)

*H*ighland Park Country Club

Auburn
Designers: Geoffrey S. Cornish
          William G. Robinson

*S*agamore Golf Club

Bolton Landing
Designer: Donald Ross

*S*chuyler Meadows Country Club

Loudonville
Designers: Devereux Emmet
Alfred H. Tull
Geoffrey S. Cornish

*T*he Hag's Fast Thinking

Walter Hagen's philosophy was "to take the game lightly, not to overplay or have golf on your mind all the time. After all, it's only a game and should be treated as one."

In a playoff with Mike Brady for the 1919 Open title, Hagen was leading by a couple of shots when he sliced his 17th tee shot to the right and the ball disappeared into a soft spot. As the gallery made a wild rush for a place beside the green, one of the spectators stepped on Hagen's ball. The ball was finally discovered two-thirds buried and black as a walnut.

After a conference, the USGA officials ruled that Hagen had to play the ball as it lay. Hagen thought for a moment, then asked, "How do I know it's my ball?" The officials were nonplussed. They had no choice but to pick it up and remove the mud before Hagen was satisfied. He lost only one stroke where he might have lost three.

*R*adisson Greens

Baldwinsville
Designers: Robert Trent Jones
Roger Rulewich

*B*artlett Country Club

Olean
Designers: Robert Trent Jones
Frank Duane

*L*eatherstocking Country Club

Cooperstown
Designer: Devereux Emmet

Judge William Cooper founded the village of Cooperstown. His son, James Fenimore Cooper, wrote the Leatherstocking Tales, chronicling the wild and dangerous life of Natty Bumppo, or "Deerslayer," one of the earliest heroes of American fiction.

The beautiful course at Cooperstown is set on the shores of Otsego Lake — in Cooper's fiction, the "Glimmerglass," where Natty himself lived.

Yahnundasis Golf Club

(right)
New Hartford
Designers: Thomas McCormick   George Low
            A.W. Leonard   Walter J. Travis

Yahnundasis was originally located on a direct trolley line from downtown Utica for the convenience of many of its charter members; among them were nine doctors who couldn't spare the travel time by horse and buggy to play golf outside the city.

Yahnundasis had courses on a succession of sites. The first was on the grounds of a hospital for infants known as Baby Hospital, where the management allowed club members to use one room as a clubhouse.

The club's first greenkeeper, Thomas McCormick of St. Andrew's in Edinburgh, Scotland, was employed on May 30, 1897, to lay out the course. McCormick must have worked fast, because on June 25, a qualifying round was played to determine eligibility for a competition slated for July!

Design fees evolved equally rapidly, if a bit later in the club's history. McCormick's fee was included in his annual salary. A.W. Leonard, who succeeded McCormick as greenkeeper and club professional, designed the second site without a specific fee, while George Low charged $25 for the third site. That modest stipend went up by twelve thousand percent when Walter Travis was hired for $3000 to expand and remodel the same site into today's highly regarded course.

From remarks by Frederick W. Owen and Sherrill Sherman at Yahnundasis 50th Anniversary Dinner, 1947

National Golf Links of America

Southampton
Designers: C.B. Macdonald
           Perry Maxwell
           Robert Trent Jones

Architect C.B. Macdonald's design for National incorporated reproductions of the best holes on the finest courses of Europe. The result was an American course hailed by many as "the greatest test of golf in the world."

72

Fresh Meadow Country Club

(left)
Great Neck
Designers: C.H. Alison   Orrin Smith
          H.S. Colt   William F. Mitchell

Author Josselyn Shore's research into the history of Fresh Meadow reveals "a fascinating story of how one man's passion for the game of golf resulted, in good measure, in the founding of both the Fresh Meadow Club and the Lakeville Golf and Country Club."

The man, Nathan Jonas, was the founder and first president of Brooklyn Jewish Hospital. He was also chairman of the board and president of Manufacturers Trust Company, and organized the Brooklyn Federation of Jewish Charities. Jonas donated land for the Lakeville course, and later, provided generous support and strong leadership to help found Fresh Meadow.

The original Fresh Meadow Country Club, designed by A.W. Tillinghast, was located in Flushing and opened in 1923. In 1925, Gene Sarazen was hired as pro. By then, Sarazen had won the U.S. Open and two PGA Championships. Earlier in his career, he had challenged Walter Hagen to a special 72-hole match for the "unofficial world championship." Sarazen won 3 and 2. After resigning as pro in 1930, he returned to Fresh Meadow to win the 1932 U.S. Open in a classic finish.

In 1946, Fresh Meadow relocated to the Village of Lake Success in Great Neck, on the site of the former Lakeville Golf and Country Club.

From *The Story of the Fresh Meadow Country Club* by Josselyn M. Shore, 1985

Wellsville Country Club

Wellsville

Springville Country Club

Springville

O*nondaga Golf & Country Club*

Fayetteville
Designers: Stanley Thompson   Phil Wogan
             Hal Purdy   Samuel Mitchell

*M*idvale Golf & Country Club

Penfield
Designers: Robert Trent Jones
Stanley Thompson

©Vince Urcioli

*P*ompey Hills Country Club

Syracuse
Designer: Hal Purdy

*S*oaring Eagles

Elmira

*C*olumbia Golf & Country Club

Hudson
Designer: Hal Purdy

*T*he Powelton Club

Newburgh
Designers: James Taylor
          Devereux Emmet   Geoffrey S. Cornish
          Robert Trent Jones   Brian Silva

The club, incorporated in 1882 as the Powelton Lawn Tennis Club, was a charter member of the U.S. Lawn Tennis Association. Golf became a formal club activity in 1895, although an anonymous historical sketch indicated that there may have been a nine-hole course on the estate before that time. Apparently, the mother-in-law of one of the members traveled to Hot Springs, Georgia, to learn how a golf course should be laid out.

Upon her return, she designed the first five holes of the course.

In September 1895, a handicap tournament ended in a tie, prompting the golf committee chairman to write to St. Andrew's Golf Club for a decision regarding the outcome. The reply: a playoff must be held. The golf committee lacked sufficient funds, however, and the tie was allowed to stand.

Durand-Eastman Park Golf Course

Rochester
Designer: Robert Trent Jones

With the founding of Genesee Valley Park, Rochester became one of the first cities in the United States to provide public golf facilities. Durand-Eastman was the city's third public course, built on park land donated in 1907 by Dr. Henry S. Durand and George Eastman, the founder of Eastman Kodak Company.

A layout of the first nine-hole course at the Park was published in Rochester's *Democrat and Chronicle* on July 14, 1918. The caption read: "You golfers who haven't gone down to Durand-Eastman Park to play on the new nine-hole course because you haven't known where to start or what direction to take if you make a start at the first tee you happened upon, here is a map of the course, the first to be published. The few enthusiasts who have played the course say it offers opportunities for all kinds of golf. It hasn't yet all that a golf course should have in the way of finish, but it is well on its way to smoothness of green and fairway, and to play on it is worthwhile. It promises to become as attractive a course as can be found in Western New York."

Ticonderoga Country Club

(left)
Ticonderoga
Designer: Seymour Dunn

The fort at Ticonderoga, which commanded the supply route between the Hudson River valley and Canada, has played an important role in American history. During the Revolutionary War, it was captured by the Green Mountain Boys under Ethan Allen and Benedict Arnold, then later retaken by British troops led by General Burgoyne. Fort Ticonderoga again fell into British hands during the French and Indian War. Near the fourth hole at the country club, a marker commemorates a skirmish of that war, fought there by soldiers on snowshoes!

From *Adirondack Golf Courses...Past and Present* by J. Peter Martin, Lake Placid, 1987

Elmira Country Club

Elmira
Designers: Willie Dunn, Jr.
          A.W. Tillinghast
          Ferdinand Garbin

The Elmira Country Club can certainly boast longevity. It is one of fewer than a dozen American golf and country clubs that have survived since the nineteenth century.

The club was founded by J. Sloat Fassett, a prominent businessman and politician, who was bitten by the golf bug during a trip to Scotland in the 1890's.

Upon his return to Elmira, a half-dozen flags reportedly appeared in holes scattered about the land outside his family home. Fassett invited friends and neighbors to try the game, and interest grew rapidly. To serve their need for an organized playing venue, Elmira Country Club was incorporated with an impressive roster of 317 charter members in 1897.

Contributed by Fred Box, Elmira

©William Oostenink

Wolferts Roost Country Club

(right)
Albany
Designer: A.W. Tillinghast

The name Wolferts Roost was derived from the works of Washington Irving and bestowed by David B. Hill, Governor of New York from 1885 to 1891, upon property he acquired from the widow of Joseph Kline Emmet, an internationally renowned actor of the post-Civil War period.

Irving had written of a Dutchman named Wolfert Acker, a privy councillor to Dutch colonial administrator Peter Stuyvesant. "He was a worthy but ill-starred man," wrote Irving, "whose aim through life had been to live in peace and quiet." When Stuyvesant was forced to surrender his domain to the British in 1664, "Wolfert retired… to the wilderness, with bitter determination to bury himself from the world." The mansion he built was called Wolferts Rust (Wolferts Rest), "but by the uneducated, who did not understand Dutch, Wolferts Roost, probably from its quaint cockloft look, and from having a weathercock perched on every gable."

Did the councillor find the serenity he sought? Local tradition has it that his wife permitted him no such bliss. Says Irving, "It soon passed into a proverb throughout the neighborhood that the cock of the Roost was the most henpecked bird in the country."

From *The History of Wolferts Roost Country Club* by Donald J. Gillen with Kathleen Burke Ford, 1985 (USGA Collection)

Seven Oaks Golf Club

Hamilton
Designers: Robert Trent Jones
         Frank Duane

Robert Trent Jones designed Seven Oaks in 1934, but the great depression intervened and the project was shelved. According to Syracuse sports writer Arnie Burdick, who interviewed Jones in 1977 at the 80th Annual NCAA Division I Collegiate Golf Championship in Hamilton, Jones "went over the land with a friend, Gene Sarazen, and laid out the course in two days. Two decades later, Colgate A.D., Eppy

Barnes, discovered the plans for the course and contacted Jones in hopes that he'd update his original undertaking. The architect immediately complied. He came to Hamilton and did some tinkering and revamping, but very little, and today's almost 7000-yard, well-watered Seven Oaks course is the result."

Nassau Country Club

(left)
Glen Cove

Designers: Devereux Emmet   Geoffrey S. Cornish
          Alfred H. Tull   Frank Duane
          Seth Raynor   George Low, Sr.
          Herbert Strong   Brian Silva

The Glen Cove, Long Island, train station was built especially for the convenience of the founding members of Nassau Country Club — millionaires like J.P. Morgan, Frederick Pratt and Henry Whitney. A beautiful red brick road once spanned the distance from the station to Nassau's magnificent stone clubhouse.

The club is the home of the "Nassau bet," a popular method of scoring friendly golf matches. Under the Nassau system, one point is awarded to the winner of each nine holes and a third point to the winner of the entire 18 holes. According to Findley S. Douglas, Nassau member and U.S. Amateur Champion of 1898, the same tycoons who thrived on high numbers all week long were somewhat sensitive when their golf scores took the same path, especially when those scores were published in the metropolitan newspapers. It wasn't long, Douglas claimed, before one of them devised a system whereby a golfer could not be beaten by more than three points.

A favorite story of long-time starter Ralph Panetta concerned Bobby Jones's fabled "Calamity Jane" putter. "Bobby Jones was staying in the neighborhood to play in the U.S. Amateur in Roslyn. He came over to shoot a round with Jim [Maiden, golf pro], complaining that his game was off. Jim loaned him a putter affectionately called Calamity Jane. Old and battered, it had a split hickory shaft that Joe Merkle, our assistant pro, had bandaged with a distinctive twine wrapping. Bobby won his first Open at Inwood in 1923 playing with that putter, and from that time on, Calamity Jane was the putter he used to win 13 national golf championships in the U.S. and Great Britain until he retired after his Grand Slam in 1930." The original Calamity Jane is now in the trophy room of the Augusta National Club. Panetta constructed a copy of the putter with its unique twining, and it now hangs over the fireplace in the club's Calamity Jane House.

Canasawacta Country Club

Norwich

*T*he Country Club of Troy

Troy
Designer: Walter J. Travis

*S*haker Ridge Country Club

Colonie
Designer: James Thomson

"In 1785 the Shakers settled in upstate New York in an attempt to escape religious persecution. The settlement known as Shaker Farms became a sacred homeland for the Shakers for over 100 years. One hundred and fifty years later the paradise founded as Shaker Farms would be the home of one of the country's premier country clubs."

From *Shaker Ridge Annual Invitational Tournament Program*

Bristol Harbor Village Golf Course

Canandaigua
Designers: Robert Trent Jones
         Rees Jones

The Country Club of Ithaca

Ithaca
Designers: Geoffrey S. Cornish
         Robert Trent Jones

The Geneva Country Club

Geneva
Designer: C.F. Crandall

The Geneva Country Club is among the oldest in the state, and one of the nation's first nine-hole golf clubs. At one time, three holes of the golf course were located on land adjacent to the club which was owned by a Mrs. Collins and included the famous Belhurst Castle. On at least one occasion, a player's limousine stopped in the club's entrance drive long enough for its chauffeur to fill a bushel basket with apples from the Collins property. Informed of the transgression, Mrs. Collins ordered her employees to plow the section of the golf course which occupied her property. It fell to the club's secretary to write a letter of apology to Mrs. Collins and restore the neighborly terms which made nine holes of golf possible at the Geneva Country Club.

From *The Geneva Country Club* by George J. Abraham, 1986 (USGA Collection)

Lakeshore Yacht & Country Club

Clay

*O*ak Hill Country Club

(right)
Rochester
Designers: Donald Ross   George Fazio
           Robert Trent Jones   Tom Fazio

Oak Hill was founded in 1901 as a nine-hole course by the Genesee River, on farmland where part of the University of Rochester now stands. In 1926 the club moved to its present home, there to build a superb Tudor clubhouse and lay out two magnificent 18-hole Donald Ross courses.

Throughout the grounds — on hillsides, terraces, lawns and lanes — stone monuments, cast memorial benches and the trunks of stately trees are set with plaques that honor the people of Oak Hill, past and present. In all, some 400 markers commemorate the League of the Iroquois, the fallen of World War II, the Women's Auxiliary, the New York Seniors Association, and other organizations and individuals.

The most famous monument is the Hill of Fame itself, where the trees on the rise forming the amphitheater to the East's 13th green are dedicated "to memorialize the immortals of golf and the distinguished citizens who have enriched the American way of life."

*G*lens Falls Country Club

Glens Falls
Designer: Donald Ross

The scenic city between Lake George and Saratoga Springs in which the Glens Falls Country Club is situated owes it name to the good sportsmanship of its founding settler, Abraham Wing. In 1763, Wing changed the name of his village from Wing's Falls to Glens Falls, after Col. Johannes Glen of Schenectady, to satisfy what the settler considered a debt of honor.

From *Golf at Glens Falls by J. Lewis Brown*, 1923 (USGA Collection)

*G*rossingers

Grossinger
Designers: Andrew Carl Salerno
            William F. Mitchell
            Joseph S. Finger

*S*hepard Hills Country Club

Waverly
Designers: Geoffrey S. Cornish
William G. Robinson

*T*he Concord Championship Course

(right)
Kiamesha Lake
Designer: Joe Finger

Dubbed "The Monster" when it first opened, this championship course wanders over 234 acres, including 34 of water, and plays 7,780 yards. However, course architect Joe Finger insists that the course was never intended to play from that length, but from its regular championship tees of 7,205 yards for the pro and 6,793 yards for the average golfer.

Just three years after its completion, the Concord course was voted into the top 20 courses in America by *Golf Digest*.

Hubie Smith, Director of Golf at the Concord, wrote that "most people, because of 'The Monster's' reputation for length and water, make the mistake of overpowering the ball, even though almost every hole is designed so that long drives demand more accuracy because the landing areas gradually narrow. Well-played shots are rewarded and poorly-played shots are penalized, but neither unduly so."

The legendary Gene Sarazen, a winner of the U.S. and British Opens, the Masters and the PGA, called the course one of "the finest built in this country."

©Fred Barden

*C*ountry Club of Buffalo

Williamsville
Designers: Donald Ross Geoffrey S. Cornish
     Robert Trent Jones William G. Robinson

Sleepy Hollow Country Club

(right)
Scarborough-on-Hudson
Designers: C.B. Macdonald
Seth Raynor   A.W. Tillinghast
Tom Winton   Robert Trent Jones

Sleepy Hollow Country Club lies in the tranquil countryside that once shuddered at the apparition of a headless horseman in Washington Irving's tale of Ichabod Crane. Diedrich Knickerbocker, a turn-of-the-century author, described this region as one of the quietest spots in the world. "If ever I should wish for a retreat," he wrote, "whither I might steal from the world and its distractions, and dream quietly away the remnant of a troubled life, I know of none more promising than this little valley."

From *The Sleepy Hollow Country Club*, 1919
(USGA Collection)

©Frank Williamson

Fort Jay Golf Club

Governors Island
Designer: Fred J. Roth

Governors Island is the only place in America where a golfer can line up a putt with the Statue of Liberty.

In 1698, this island just off Manhattan was "set aside...as part of the Denison of His Majestie's Fort at New York for the benefit of His Majestie's Governors." With the English evacuation in 1783, the American Army took possession of Governors Island; today the Coast Guard manages it.

Around 1800, Fort Jay, a latter-day recreation of a medieval fortification with moats, a sally port, drawbridge and postern gate, was completed on

Governors Island and armed with 100 guns. Today the fort plays a prominent part in one of the most unique golf courses in America; the moat, for instance, has become a rather unusual hazard, and cannon balls from a bombardment by Admiral Howe's fleet are sometimes discovered on the grounds.

More recently, Governors Island gained international notice as the site of a luncheon hosted by President and Mrs. Reagan for Soviet leader Mikhail Gorbachev and his wife during their U.S. visit near the close of the Reagan presidency.

96

©William S. Sovik

A Difference of Opinion

[Golf] consists of putting a little white ball into a little hole with instruments very ill-adapted for the purpose.

Winston Churchill

[Golf] is a science — the study of a lifetime, in which you may exhaust yourself but never your subject. It is a contest, a duel or melee calling for courage, skill, strategy and self-control. It is a test of temper, a trial of honor, a revealer of character. It affords the chance to play the man and act the gentleman. It means going into God's out-of-doors, getting close to nature, fresh air, exercise, a sweeping away of the mental cobwebs, general recreation of the tired tissues. It is a cure for care — an antidote for worry. It includes companionship with friends, social intercourse, opportunity for courtesy, kindliness and generosity to an opponent. It promotes not only physical health but mental force.

David R. Forgan, Scottish golfer and clubmaker (ca. 1890)

Contributing Photographers

Linda Bishop McCarthy
Jules Alexander
Fred Barton
David Earl
Leonard Kamsler
MGA Collection
Bryan McCallen
William Oostenink
William S. Sovik
Vince Urcioli
Frank Williamson